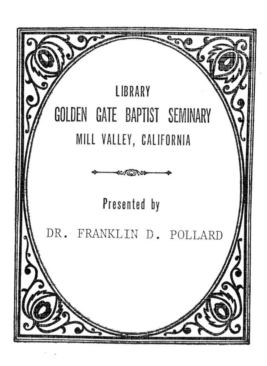

Candles in the Dark

CANDLES IN THE DARK

MAE HURLEY ASHWORTH

BROADMAN PRESS
Nashville, Tennessee

1983

Dedication

In memory of Ursula
who lit many candles

Preface

On November 9, 1965, a massive power failure blacked out most of the northeastern United States and parts of two Canadian provinces. At the time, I was living in New York, one of the cities affected.

A friend and I were riding home from work on a bus late that afternoon when we were amazed to see the lights of Manhattan go out one by one. The city which had gleamed with a radiance which gave it the nickname "Baghdad on the Hudson" suddenly became a pit of blackness, lit only intermittently by the headlights of cars.

Expecting the blackout to be of short duration, we stopped off at a restaurant, which was soon jammed with others in the same situation. Several hours later we realized that we were caught, like millions of New Yorkers, in a crisis of major proportions. The buses had stopped running, and we would have to find our way home on foot through the dark streets.

The experience could have been terrifying, but it was not. New Yorkers, for the most part, responded to the crisis as though their lives were dedicated to helping others. Car rides were offered and flashlights shared. Ablebodied people assisted those who were frailer in crossing streets. The sharp-eyed steered those of poorer vision. Hotels and restaurants offered shelter to many who could not make it home. One of my friends slept on the floor of a restaurant with a pillow provided by the proprietor. And as the crowds moved through the dark streets they joked together, cheering one another on.

Yet I remember most gratefully the candles which began to appear in the windows of stores and apartments. Unable to emblazon the city with the huge lights which would have dispelled the darkness, people offered the frail radiance of their candles to guide the struggling homeseekers. There was a wealth of comfort in the tiny flames, for we knew that behind them were people who cared and on whom we could call for help if need be.

Those candles became for me a symbol of the small acts of faith, love, and kindness that often seem trifling but which, in their cumulative effect, give life a quality of beauty it would not otherwise have. I have observed many such acts in my life and have heard of countless others. Some of them are recorded in this book. These stories, not about great missions, major projects, or deeds that shook the world, are about *candles in the dark*.

Contents

An Introduction to America

I was a stranger and you welcomed me (Matt. 25:35).

Mrs. A., a Frenchwoman, had lived in this country for some years before I met her, but she told me a moving story about her first week here.

She and her husband had come to New York to attend to some business interests and had rented an apartment in Brooklyn. Within a few days of their arrival, Mr. A. suffered a heart attack and died almost immediately.

Distraught, alone, and without friends in a strange land, Mrs. A. was frantic. Hardly realizing what she was doing, she rushed to the street to seek help.

Mr. W., a businessman of the neighborhood who happened to be passing by, saw her and realized that something was wrong. He spoke to her and asked if he could help.

When she sobbed out the story of her predicament, he returned to the apartment with her and called a doctor. After the fact of death had been confirmed Mr. W. took charge of the funeral arrangements, accompanying Mrs. A. to a mortician and notifying a minister of her faith.

On the day of the interment, only Mrs. A., Mr. W., and the minister stood at the graveside. But when the service was completed and Mrs. A. turned away, she was amazed to see standing nearby a small group of people. Mr. W. had

11

notified other neighborhood businessmen that a lonely woman was burying her husband, and they had come—the butcher, the grocer, the haberdasher, and their wives—to support her in her time of grief.

It was her introduction to the great heart of America.

Dear Father, Let me never forget to show kindness to strangers, for your love is theirs as well as mine, and I want to be your instrument in expressing it. In Jesus' name, Amen.

My Gloves and Justice

He is our peace, who has made us both one, and has broken down the dividing wall of hostility (Eph. 2:14).

I was about to step off a bus one day when a cry behind me stopped me in my tracks. "Lady, lady! Wait a minute!"

When I looked around, I saw a young black woman racing after me, waving a pair of gloves in the air—mine. I had dropped them as I left my seat.

I took the gloves, thanked the woman, and went on my way, wondering at the marvel of human capacity for love. I thought of the years when black people in this country were denied many of the basic rights we had boasted our democracy gave to everyone. I was aware, as my benefactor must have been, that some whites still begrudge blacks their place in the sun. She had no way of knowing that I was not one of them. Yet without hesitation she had offered me her help.

Then I remembered that through all the sorrowful years blacks had clung to their church, learning faith, love, and

forgiveness. Miraculously, black Christians had been able to see good even in those who wronged them.

For whites, too, faith finally led to the imperative for justice, and the walls began to tumble.

Dear Father, Bless all who forgive and all who repent. Open the hearts of those not yet reconciled, that our society may be whole again. In Jesus' name, Amen.

Eight Cents of Goodwill

Blessed is he who considers the poor! (Ps. 41:1).

I was in a convenience store, waiting my turn to be served. Immediately ahead of me was a frail, shabbily-dressed elderly man. He placed several small items on the counter and handed the clerk a dollar.

"It's a dollar eight with the tax," said the clerk.

The old man stared at him dazedly, without speaking.

"Do you have the other eight cents?"

Before the old man could reply a second clerk at the counter, a teenaged girl, said softly, "It's all right. I have eight cents I can put in for him."

The other clerk nodded. "Sure. The two of us can take care of it."

He put the old man's purchases into a bag and handed it to him. Grasping the bag, the old man muttered his thanks and started for the door.

"Have a good day!" the two young clerks called after him.

Those words, so often spoken mechanically, in this

instance took on warm meaning. The young people had just demonstrated their genuine concern.

Often we read about how some wealthy person has established a scholarship for a needy student or given a princely sum to a center for the elderly. Sighing, we think, "If only I could do something like that!"

But charity does not need a million dollars. Sometimes it only needs eight cents—and love.

Dear Father, Give me quick eyes and ears to sense any situation in which even my token help can make a good day for someone who needs me. In Jesus' name, Amen.

"I Had to Call My Dad"

Lo, sons are a heritage from the Lord (Ps. 127:3).

I was in a coffee shop when word came over the radio that a heavy storm was brewing and would soon sweep over the city.

A young counterman, a look of concern on his face, stopped what he was doing and hurried to the back of the restaurant. Presently he returned, smiling.

"I had to call my dad," he explained. "He goes out for a walk every afternoon, and I didn't want him to get caught in the storm. He's been sick lately, and it might set him back."

I thought about the love and concern represented by that telephone call. A son so anxious for his father's well-being would surely be kind and considerate in every way.

In these days when we talk about the generation gap and

read about families torn apart by antagonism, it is good to know that loving family relationships still exist, with sons and daughters who hold it a prime responsibility to care for the parents who nurtured them. God instituted the family for our comfort and happiness, and loving children are truly among his greatest gifts.

Dear Father, Help us always to remember our responsibilities, parent to child and child to parent. Let us, in love, cleave to the family circle you gave us. In Jesus' name, Amen.

The Sharp Eyes of Love

This is my commandment, that you love one another as I have loved you (John 15:12).

Some people seem to enjoy rushing breathlessly about their own business. My temperament makes me prefer taking things at a more leisurely pace. I like the pause that makes the next step easier.

One day, climbing a double flight of stairs in a subway station, I stopped on the landing after the first flight to catch my breath. Dozens of people streamed by as I rested there. Finally, however, a woman stopped, and with a look of concern on her face asked, "Are you all right?"

I thanked her and assured her that I was. After she walked on I regretted that I had not told her that her concern had, nonetheless, been important to me. I hadn't needed help at that moment, but I—and many other people—might someday. It was good to know that in the hustle and bustle of a mammoth city there are people with the sharp eyes of love who are quick to spot someone who might be in distress.

Dear Father, Thank you for the thoughtful people who do not pass by when there is need or potential need. Help me to be one of them. In Jesus' name, Amen.

A Hint of Calvary

Greater love has no man than this, that a man lay down his life for his friends (John 15:13).

Mr. C., a gifted man who was expected to have a brilliant future, was returning home one night when he saw a teenage boy being beaten by a gang of thugs. Without hesitation he rushed to the rescue. He succeeded in driving off the attackers and saving the boy, but not before he himself was fatally injured. He died in a hospital a short time later.

Some of his friends felt, bitterly, that the sacrifice was not worth it. Was the boy's life worth more than his—or as much? Was he responsible for the public protection that we expect from the police?

These are hard questions, but I think that if Mr. C. could have replied he might have said that no man who values his own life can fail to value that of another. Had he lived, his gifts might have meant much to many, but nothing he could ever have done would have provided a brighter inspiration

than his affirmation that night of the brotherhood of man.

Dear Father, Give me the courage, if need should arise, to face danger in order to shield another. In Jesus' name, Amen.

Bringing Us Together

Agree with one another, live in peace (2 Cor. 13:11).

Two teenage boys, one black and one white, entered a restaurant where I was having coffee and sat down near me. They were carrying on an animated conversation, laughing and jostling each other, evidently in good spirits. The conversation, however, was soundless, conducted with their flying fingers. They were deaf mutes.

As I watched them, noting the pleasure they took in their companionship, I was aware of an important element in their friendship. These youngsters could have been divided by their color, as so many people are, but the likeness they shared in their mutual handicap had brought them together.

Surely there is a message here for all of us. We tend to make too much of the differences between our neighbors and ourselves. Differences of color, politics, religious interpretations, and even such minor matters as taste in food and entertainment often make us draw away from individuals who could enrich our lives. We need to discover the likenesses we share as God's creatures and members of the human family. The key is to approach others with a determination to uncover our mutual aims, desires, and needs, which are sure to be more numerous than our differences.

Dear Father, Help me relate to others in a positive way, seeking likeness in the face of difference. In Jesus' name, Amen.

"Help Me Keep My Cool"

The Lord is my strength and my song (Ps. 118:14).

Enjoying a quiet meal in a restaurant, I heard a loud, angry voice at the next table berating the waitress because a meal had not been cooked to satisfaction.

There was a moment's pause and then the waitress spoke politely. "I'm so sorry. I'll try to get you another serving."

There was no hint of a sharp edge in the words. I wondered at the young woman's patience.

Later, when the other customer had left, I asked the waitress how she managed to cope so sweetly with unreasonable diners and said teasingly, "Do you count to ten before you speak?"

She laughed. "No, I stop long enough to say in my head, 'Dear God, please help me keep my cool.'"

I looked at her fresh, untroubled young face and was glad she had acquired such early wisdom. Many of us forget, when our encounters with others are difficult, that there is a Source of gentleness that we can tap.

Dear Father, Thank you for the strength and patience you give us to control our emotions in times of trial. Help us remember that kindness is better than anger. In Jesus' name, Amen.

Getting Turned into Giving

I will gather yet others to him besides those already gathered (Isa. 56:8).

In the neighborhood of a church I once attended lived Mr. Y., an old man whose days were spent in a shuttle between his small, rented room and a park bench. His source of income was unknown, but certainly quite meager.

One day as several church women were preparing for a fellowship supper, Mr. Y. appeared at the kitchen door and asked hesitantly if he might have a cup of coffee. The women immediately invited him in and suggested that he stay for the meal. Shyly he refused, but accepted a piece of cake and the coffee he had asked for.

That was the beginning of a regular association. Whenever the church kitchen was in use, Mr. Y. seemed to know. He would come for his coffee and chat for a while with the cooks. But when invited to join in the services or activities of the church, he became evasive.

Then Mr. Y. was struck by a car and hospitalized. He was not seriously injured, but because the driver had been clearly at fault Mr. Y. was paid a substantial amount in damages. As soon as he received the money, he came to our pastor and announced his intention of giving a gift to the church.

It happened that just at this time the church was raising funds to help Mr. S., an elderly member who wanted to enter a retirement home where he was required to make a down payment he could not afford. The pastor suggested that Mr. Y. might like to contribute to this fund, and he was delighted with the idea.

When we held a small, farewell get-together for Mr. S.,

Mr. Y. was present. Having become a giver as well as a receiver, he was ready to become one of us.

Dear Father, Help us to give without making demands, leaving it to your spirit to complete the circle of love. In Jesus' name, Amen.

A Child's Christmas Sacrifice

It is more blessed to give than to receive (Acts 20:35).

On the day before the closing of school for the Christmas holidays, many of the children in my class brought gifts for me. The youngsters gathered around my desk to watch me open the bright packages.

As I exclaimed with appreciation when each gift came into view, I noticed little Millie on the edge of the group, her eyes wistful. She had brought no gift, because her family could not afford the luxury of such giving. With a sad lack of understanding, I thought she coveted the pretty scarf I had just unwrapped.

Presently she walked quietly back to her desk. When she returned, she was clutching a bookmark in the shape of a golden kitten. It was her treasure. I had seen her fondle it and show it proudly to the other children.

She held it out. "This is for you."

For a moment I felt sheer dismay. How could I take this from her when she had so little? But I knew I could not refuse, for that would have been a cruel rejection.

My throat tight, I said, "Thank you, Millie. This is one of the nicest gifts I have ever received."

Many of our gifts are bought with dollars we don't need, for people who don't need them and will probably return gifts of similar value. Millie's gift was of another order, a sacrifice in the true spirit of Christmas.

Dear Father, Help me learn that there are times when I should put aside my own needs, my own desires, and my own comfort to give joy to others. I know that the spirit of sacrifice is the spirit of love and brings me closer to you, who sacrificed your Son for the world. In Jesus' blessed name, Amen.

How a Businessman Should Behave

Repay no one evil for evil, but take thought for what is noble in the sight of all (Rom. 12:17).

Miss L. had been secretary for some years to a business executive Mr. R., she revered. I understood her devotion after hearing her tell the following story:

"Mr. R. had a rival, Mr. W., who was completely unscrupulous. He did everything he could to destroy Mr. R.'s business, even spreading a false rumor that the product Mr. R. manufactured was defective.

"Then a fire destroyed Mr. W.'s warehouse, consuming his entire inventory of goods. Without money to replace his stock, he was facing ruin. His past practices had made banks unwilling to advance him a loan.

"Abjectly, he came to Mr. R. for help. I was present at the interview and expected righteous wrath to descend on Mr. W.'s head. But when Mr. W. pleaded, 'If you could only give me an advance for a few months, I could make it,' Mr.

R. asked quietly, 'How much do you need?' and wrote a check.

"After Mr. W. left the office, I asked in amazement, 'How on earth could you help that man, when he's treated you so abominably?'

"After a moment's hesitation Mr. R. replied, eyes twinkling, 'Oh, maybe I just wanted to show him how a businessman should behave.'"

Miss L., however, was sure that the reasons went deeper. "I saw in his eyes that he felt sorry for the man. I've never known anyone with so much compassion."

Dear Father, Let me not reserve my compassion for those who have earned it. Let me offer it as a free gift, even as our Lord offered himself for a sinful world. In Christ's name, Amen.

Kindness in Relationships

A man who is kind benefits himself (Prov. 11:17).

During a train ride some years ago I fell into conversation with a man who shared my seat. He had recently made a decision and was not sure he had done the right thing. He wanted my opinion.

His son, a high-school football player, had brought a teammate, a black boy, home for dinner. The man and his wife, who had grown up in a community where segregation of the races was an unbreakable rule, were thrown into a state of panic. They retreated to the kitchen to talk over the situation.

"Finally," he said, "we decided we'd just have to go

through with it. We couldn't bear to hurt the kid's feelings."

I assured him that I thought he had done the right thing and added that I myself had black friends with whom I had not only shared many meals but also worship, work, and recreation.

I felt a deep sympathy and rapport with this man. All of us whites who grew up in the first half of the century were brainwashed to believe in racial inequality, and the way out of such conditioning is not easy. But my companion had taken the first step and was on his way. An individual who doesn't want to hurt anyone has a head start in human relationships. I knew that in time he'd go beyond not wanting to hurt and begin to help in the great movement toward racial equality.

Dear Father, Let all my human relationships be guided by the wish to help and not hurt. In Jesus' name, Amen.

The Truth Doesn't Have to Hurt

But if anyone has caused pain, . . . turn to forgive and comfort him, or he may be overwhelmed with excessive sorrow (2 Cor. 2:5-6).

"We should learn to use the truth sparingly," said one of my cleverest friends.

Knowing her to be a completely truthful woman, I was astonished.

She laughed at the expression on my face. "I don't mean that we should lie," she said. "It's just that we shouldn't use the truth as a club to beat people. Sometimes, when telling someone an unpleasant truth would hurt him deeply, we need to keep our mouths shut."

A few weeks later, I saw her philosophy in action. The two of us were attending the funeral of an elderly woman whose daughter, Miss G., was known for her peppery temper. As we left the church, a woman muttered to us, "If Miss G. hadn't flown out at her mother all the time, she wouldn't have to cry so much now. Somebody ought to tell her that."

My friend said quickly, "Oh, no, I think she already knows. Did you notice her face?"

Later, my friend found the opportunity to tell Miss G., "I remember the lovely party you gave for your mother on her eightieth birthday. I'm sure you'll always be glad you made her happy that day."

Dear Father, It is easy to see the faults of others, and sometimes I may be tempted to speak cruel truths. Help me to govern my tongue so that it speaks those truths that are healing and helpful. In Jesus' name, Amen.

Warm Hearts at a Fire

There are varieties of working, but it is the same God who inspires them all in every one (1 Cor. 12:6).

One evening a fire broke out in a building complex near the apartment house where I live. It raged on through the night, with weary fire fighters working in relays taking short periods of rest in turn.

A woman from our building, passing by, saw that the fire

fighters had no place to relax, no means of refreshment. As soon as she reached home she organized a relief team among our tenants. A table was brought into the lobby and a large coffee urn appeared, soon chuckling and steaming with a fragrant brew. Platters of sandwiches and cookies were brought from various apartments. Then a messenger was dispatched to invite the fire fighters to spend their rest periods as guests of the house.

It was heartwarming to see exhausted fire fighters, faces smudged with soot, stumble in and then, after a cheering cup of coffee and a snack, return to work with a jauntier step.

One of them commented, as he left, "You ladies are real fire fighters, yes ma'am!"

It's a privilege to be able to show appreciation to the people—fire fighters, police, sanitation men, and others—whose service keeps our cities and towns livable. Recognition of the need all of us have for others under God's good plan is the cement that holds communities together.

Dear God, Let me remember to be grateful for the benefits you have provided through others for my well-being. May my thanks be expressed to you and to them. In Jesus' name, Amen.

The Courage to Answer "I Can"

I give you what I have (Acts 3:6).

A widow with several children married a man who had lost both legs in an accident. Mr. T., despite his handicap, was an industrious employed person who never bewailed his misfortune nor considered himself unable to carry the full responsibilities of a husband and father. Mrs. T. and her youngsters were happy with him for a year and then, unexpectedly, she died.

Neighbors and friends assumed that Mr. T. would give up the children. Why should a man in his situation undertake the care of children not his own, without the help of a wife?

Instead, he gathered them around him, assuring them of his continuing love and his intention to care for them until they were able to face the world on their own.

Mr. T. must give pause to all of us who, at one time or another, have used our particular weaknesses as excuses to shirk responsibility. The truth is, of course, that everyone is handicapped in one way or another. No one is endowed with every possible gift. But if we give what we have in service, refusing to believe it is not enough, it can become a greater blessing than we ever dared hope.

Dear Father, Give me the courage to say "I can" when I am needed. In the Master's name, Amen.

A Postman's Service

Bear one another's burdens, and so fulfil the law of Christ (Gal. 6:2).

Mrs. W., a widow, is almost blind, and she lives alone. One day when the postman handed her a letter, she commented wistfully, "I won't know what's in it until one of my friends comes by to read it to me."

The postman answered promptly, "I'll be glad to come in

and read it for you, if you'd like for me to."

Gratefully she accepted his offer, and a fruitful relationship began. From that time on, whenever Mrs. W. had mail the postman acted as her reader. The result was a rare friendship.

That postman knew that a job is not merely a job. It is a service to one's fellow human beings. Where there is special need, the conscientious workman responds with the help required. In his code, there is no such thing as, "It isn't my responsibility."

Dear Father, Whether at work or play, let me see another's need as my responsibility and my opportunity. In Jesus' name, Amen.

Preserving a Life

Give, and it shall be given unto you (Luke 6:38, KJV).

Ralph, a young man driving through a strange community, was involved in a near-fatal collision. In serious condition, he needed massive transfusions of blood. The small local hospital, caught without sufficient reserves, issued a plea for help by radio to the town's residents.

The response was overwhelming. Among the throng of would-be donors, enough were found with the right blood type to supply Ralph's needs. Thanks to this unhesitating compassion, he made a complete recovery.

When he learned about the community effort that had saved him, he was deeply moved. He sat down and wrote a letter of thanks to each donor. One line read, "Your blood is in my veins helping me to live, and I love you for it."

A man who received this heartfelt expression of gratitude said, "That guy did as much for me as I did for him. To know that I'd helped save a human life was the greatest feeling I've ever had."

Anyone who has experienced the feeling of having helped save another from disaster knows that there is no greater reward. However small his contribution may have been, he is aware that he has worked with God to help preserve the precious spark of life.

Dear Father, As you have given us life, let me be among those who help preserve and beautify it. In Jesus' name, Amen.

Being a Friend

A friend loves at all times (Prov. 17:17).

Due to a sudden changeover in the management of her company, Eleanor had just lost her job. The dismissal had come without warning, after many years of devoted work, and it was a traumatic experience. Eleanor was in a state of shock and dismay.

Desperately in need of company, she called a friend. The friend listened to her outpouring for a few minutes and then said briskly, "Now keep your chin up. It isn't the end of the world. I'm sorry I can't talk any longer, but I have an appointment in about fifteen minutes. I'll see you tomorrow."

The phone clicked, and Eleanor stood beside it trembling. Tears filling her eyes, she dialed again.

"Louise? I've just lost my job. I need to talk to someone. Could you . . . ?"

The voice from the other end of the line came warmly over the wires. "Hold everything, Honey. I'll be right over."

Shortly afterward Louise arrived, carrying two cartons of hot coffee and some sandwiches she had picked up at the delicatessen.

"Now let's have a bite and talk about it."

Through a long evening Louise listened while Eleanor poured out her fears. Jobs were scarce, and she was past the age considered most desirable for employment. What could she do?

Louise countered by reminding her of her fine skills, asking Eleanor to hold on to her faith that God still had a plan for her life. Gradually Eleanor became calmer and more cheerful. Hope came back as a balm she had forgotten.

Later, when she was reemployed she said of that evening, "Without her I would have gone to pieces."

Sometimes ministering to the needs of a friend in trouble requires that we drop everything else, putting their priorities before our own.

Dear Father, When my friends need me, give me the grace to be there. As you always hear me, let me also hear their pleas for comfort. In Jesus' name, Amen.

The Ten-cent Pumpkin

The mind of the wise makes his speech judicious (Prov. 16:23).

It was the week before Halloween, and I was in a grocery with a friend.

A small boy burst in, rushed up to the counter, and asked happily, "I want the biggest pumpkin you have for a dime!"

The grocery clerk guffawed. "Well, boy, I'm afraid my biggest pumpkins cost a lot more than that."

Most of the people in the store joined in his laughter. The little boy's face grew red, and he stammered, "I didn't mean . . . I meant . . . " He faltered, and stood helplessly looking at the dime in his hand.

My friend stepped up beside him. "He meant," she said firmly, "that he would like to buy the biggest pumpkin you are able to sell for a dime."

The matter explained, the little boy bought his pumpkin and left the store, cradling the prize carefully in his arms.

Children often have trouble expressing their precise meanings, and adults need to be sensitive, as my friend was, to look for the idea behind the words. It is easy to laugh and erase the smile from an eager young face, harder to be understanding and keep it in place.

Dear Father, When I deal with small children give me a sensitive heart and a wise tongue, so that no thoughtlessness of mine shall mar their happiness. In Jesus' lovely name, Amen.

He Failed—Only to Succeed

Each has his own special gift from God, one of one kind and one of another (1 Cor. 7:7).

Mr. H. was, judged by the usual standards, a sorry failure. The son of a wealthy and distinguished family, he was the one member of the brood who had not inherited the brilliance of the others.

All during his growing-up years he struggled to overcome his lack of gifts, but the odds were against him. When he became a man, his successful siblings dispatched him to my hometown with seed money for the start of a small business.

His business venture creaked along for a number of years, sometimes breaking even but often losing money. By the time Mr. H. reached old age it had failed completely, and he was financially strapped.

Reduced to living in a shack in the poorest district of town, Mr. H. never lost his dignity or gave evidence of self-pity. Instead, he interested himself in the people around him and made them his friends. He noticed particularly a little girl next door, under whose mop of unkempt hair he discovered a bright mind and lively spirit.

Despite his lack of cleverness, Mr. H. had enjoyed the benefits of an excellent education. He used it to help the child who had the native ability he lacked but had never known the stimulating environment to which he had been born. He became her tutor, helping her not only with her school work but also with lessons in grooming and manners. Her full potential realized, she developed into a lovely and productive person.

All of us who saw the transformed life Mr. H. made possible gained a new perspective on failure and success. The finest success, we realized, means doing what we are able to do in the place where we are to make life better for those around us.

Dear Father, Let me not scorn the gifts you have given me, small though they may be. Help me to find the place for them, that others may be blessed. In the Name above every name, Amen.

A Generous Spirit

In humility count others better than yourselves (Phil. 2:3).

I was in church waiting for the service to begin when an old man came down the aisle and entered the pew where I was sitting. After he had pushed past me with great effort, I realized how inconsiderate I had been. I had practically forced him to climb over my knees when I could just as easily have slid along the seat to make room for him.

When the service was over I turned toward him to apologize. Before I could speak he said gently, "Please excuse me for coming in late, Miss, and pushing past you like that. I should have been earlier."

I experienced a surge of pleasure, not because I no longer felt at fault (for I assured him that I had been thoughtless) but because it was a joy to meet so generous-spirited a person. Having been inconvenienced, he looked for the cause in his own actions rather than in mine.

It is easy to assess others with blame for the irritations and hurts we experience. When we are jostled or pushed, we are apt to think, "What a rude person!" We may forget to consider that perhaps we were standing in a place that made passage difficult for others. When someone speaks to us sharply, we are shocked by that person's ill humor and may fail to ask ourselves, "Did I say or do something that would have tried the patience of a saint?"

Dear Father, When I am hurt or inconvenienced by other persons, help me to turn the situation inside out and look at it as they may see it. If I am to blame, even in part, let me have the grace to acknowledge my fault. In Jesus' name, Amen.

Faith Accents the Positive

He who is slow to anger quiets contention (Prov. 15:18).

A celebrity once told an interviewer about what she called her hardest struggle. She had found herself the target of gossip columnists whose stories were often untrue, biased, and unfair. She was becoming angry and bitter. She found herself suspicious of everyone she met, wondering what they might report about her.

Finally she asked herself whether her faith permitted her such rage and negativism. She decided to take herself in hand. From that day on, whenever she read something unpleasant about herself, she sat down and wrote out her feelings about the story. She then crumpled up the paper and threw it into the wastebasket. The matter had been disposed of, and she put it out of her mind.

One day at a party she encountered a man she had known pleasantly several years before. She greeted him warmly. It was not until she saw the startled expression on his face that she remembered his changed attitude toward her and the fact that he had been a severe critic.

The rift was healed, and he never again wrote unkindly about her.

All of us would like to better human relationships by correcting the faults of others, but often the only place to begin is with ourselves.

Dear Father, Help me to forget slights and remember favors so that my heart will always be open to reconciliation. In Jesus' name, Amen.

We're Only Human

Love is patient and kind (1 Cor. 13:4).

Linda was only eighteen and living nervously through her first day as cashier in a restaurant. She tells it this way:

"I've always been good at arithmetic, but that day I couldn't add two and two or tell a nickel from a dime. I kept making stupid mistakes, and I got plenty of dirty looks. This scared me even more, and I made more mistakes.

"When a man came along and gave me a five-dollar bill to pay for a three-twenty-five check, I gave him a dollar and a quarter in change. He smiled and said, 'I think you owe me fifty cents more.' I was so excited that when I scooped up two quarters I dropped one of them, and as I bent to pick it up I bumped my head on the cash register. By that time I was a basket case, ready to cry and scream. But the man just smiled at me nicely, as if nothing important had happened.

"'Sorry I got you rattled,' he said, 'everybody makes mistakes, so it's no big deal.'

"He sounded so sincere that I calmed down immediately. I'd been feeling like the dumbest girl in the world, but he'd made me realize that I was just human."

Sometimes when we are in a hurry we become irritated with people who seem inefficient. We can't always know their problems or why they flub simple transactions. Yet we need to bear with them in charity, as we hope others will do when we make mistakes.

Dear Father, Help me to be understanding when others inconvenience me with their human failings, as I wish to be understood when I am the one at fault. In Jesus' name, Amen.

A Stepmother's Love

Who shall separate us from the love of Christ? (Rom. 8:35).

"How is your stepmother feeling?" a friend asked Jean one day when the lady in question was slightly ill.

"She's doing fine," replied Jean, "but please don't call her my stepmother. There's no step between my mother and me."

Jean often spoke glowingly of the woman she refused to call her stepmother. Her natural mother had died when she was quite small, and when her father remarried she felt a timid child's uncertainty about what her life might be in the hands of the strange female who had come into her home.

The new mother soon dispelled these fears. On the first day she said to Jean confidingly, "Jean, you've known your father a lot longer than I have. You'll have to help me learn how to take the best care of him. What do you think he'd like for dinner tonight?"

Jean never forgot the feeling of pride and reassurance those words gave her. She was to be treated as the heart of the home, not as someone to be pushed aside now that a new member had come into the family. That pattern would persist through the years.

"She wasn't a softie," Jean pointed out. "She corrected me when I needed it, but I always knew she loved me and cared about everything that made me happy. She was my mother with a capital *M*."

Stories abound of wicked stepmothers and foster homes where children are brutally mistreated. They are sometimes tragically true, and because they make dramatic reading they receive wide press coverage. But all over the earth quieter stories are being played out by stepchildren and adopted children who have found comfort in the homes of new parents. The love that surrounds and protects them leaves no step to divide them from the care God meant all children to enjoy.

Dear Father, Thank you for every man and woman who has reached out to give a child the feeling of belonging in a family circle of love. Grant that each receives in return the love that was given. In Jesus' glorious name, Amen.

Enjoying Others' Success

Rejoice with those who rejoice, weep with those who weep (Rom. 12:15).

I was visiting with Ann one day when her telephone rang. She left the room to answer it, and when she came back she was smiling happily.

"It was Helen," she said, naming one of her neighbors. "She wanted to tell me that Jim [Helen's son] got that engineering job he applied for. Isn't it great? I'd been hoping and praying that he would."

I was not surprised that Helen had called to share her good news. She knew that Ann would rejoice with her, as she always rejoiced at the successes of others. It was the special gift of a spirit without envy.

We have a scornful name for those who desert their friends in time of need. We call them fair-weather friends. Perhaps there should be a comparable name—foul-weather friends—for those who, smug in their own happiness, are able to console the sorrowful but are unable to enjoy wholeheartedly the good fortune of others. Genuine love requires that we be at one with our fellows in both sorrow and joy.

Dear Father, Never let envy make my love falter. Help me increase the joy of others by adding to it my own. For Jesus' sake, Amen.

In-laws—Not Outlaws

Your people shall be my people, and your God my God (Ruth 1:16).

A young wife confessed, "The first year I was married my mother-in-law and I were like two cats with our backs humped. It seemed to me that she couldn't get over the idea that she was the leading lady in John's life and the only one who could look after him. I resented every suggestion she made, and she made a lot of them.

"Finally I realized that we were making John terribly unhappy, and I felt I had to do something about it. The next time we went to my mother-in-law's for dinner, she had a marvelous raisin pie, and John raved about how good it was. I began getting uptight, thinking maybe he liked her cooking better than mine. Then I just made myself smile and say, 'It really is super. Could I have the recipe? I wish I could cook the way you do.'

"She looked as if she couldn't believe her ears, but I could tell she was pleased. From that day on, I began to ask her advice about things. Of course I didn't do everything her way, but I did show that I appreciated her suggestions. We get along fine now, and believe it or not, sometimes she asks my advice."

The Bible tells us to honor our fathers and mothers. I believe, by extension, we are expected to include the parents of our mates. Certainly, the story of Ruth and Naomi would inspire us to make our relationship with them one of love and respect.

Dear Father, Give me the grace to overlook small irritations and avoid petty jealousies that would keep me from loving relationships with those close to me. In Jesus' name, Amen.

The Blessed Bicycle

God is able to provide . . . in abundance for every good work (2 Cor. 9:8).

Mrs. H. taught a class of retarded and mostly under-privileged children. One of the little boys in her class talked obsessively about his longing for a bicycle. He seemed to believe that somehow, sometime, he would get one, but Mrs. H. knew his parents would never be able to afford anything so expensive.

When Kenny's birthday approached, Mrs. H. wished with all her heart that she could make him happy with the gift of a bicycle. The idea seemed impossible, for she had two children of her own, and the financial situation in her home was tight. Yet she was unable to dismiss the notion from her mind. She thought about it every time she was near a store where bicycles were sold.

One day, in an unfamiliar neighborhood, she passed a secondhand store. There in the window stood a gleaming bicycle, looking brand new and intact. Almost trembling with eagerness, Mrs. H. went inside to look at it. Close examination proved it to be in perfect condition.

To her amazement, the price was less than a fourth of what a new bicycle would have cost. Apparently some child had tired of it, and his parents had disposed of it at a fraction of its cost.

Mrs. H.'s problem was solved. She could hardly believe her good luck. But was it luck? She didn't think so.

"I'm sure it was intended that I find that bicycle," she said, "and for Kenny to have it, with the caring it represented to him. The look on his face when he saw it is something I'll never forget."

Dear Father, I know that you are able to guide and prosper us when our purposes are good. Help me to accomplish all my wishes that are kind and just. In Jesus' name, Amen.

The Gift of Peacemaking

Blessed are the peacemakers, for they shall be called sons of God (Matt. 5:9).

As a small child I had a playmate named Mary. We were devoted friends; but sometimes, like all youngsters, we became cross with each other.

One day, playing with blocks at her house, we built a tall, rather wobbly tower. For some reason that I can't remember, when the work was finished I gave the structure a little push, and the blocks came tumbling down.

Mary objected and spoke to me sharply. Within minutes we were quarreling at the top of our voices.

The door opened, and Mary's mother came in. We fell silent, expecting to be scolded, but she only said quietly,

"How would you girls like some nice, fresh strawberries?"

As we dipped into a dishful of sweet fruit topped by cream, Mary and I were completely restored to good humor. A kind woman—one of the best I have ever known—had made peace without a lecture.

I have since known other gifted peacemakers. One, a calm, poised woman who chaired a church committee, always awed me with her ability to bring conflicting views together. When an argument grew shrill she uncannily chose and stressed the points on which antagonists could agree, showing them that both really wanted to further in the best possible way the project at hand.

For men and women of goodwill, the real struggle is to learn to work together in love.

Dear Father, Give me the gift of peace and the ability to share it with others. In Jesus' name, Amen.

The Tonic of Appreciation

Therefore encourage one another and build one another up (1 Thess. 5:11).

As a young teacher, I often felt tired and discouraged. Trying to meet the needs of more than thirty children with assorted problems sometimes led to frustration.

One day I went home so exhausted and beaten that I felt I never wanted to see my classroom again. As I sat indulging in a bit of self-pity, the telephone rang.

An enthusiastic voice came over the wires. "I just wanted to tell you how much I appreciate that booklet you had the children make about their own experiences. I think it's the finest thing Virginia has ever done in school."

I thanked the thoughtful mother who had called, but I'm sure she could not possibly know what she did for me that day. Not only had she turned discouragement into a sense of achievement, but she had made me aware for the rest of my life of how important appreciation can be.

Years later, I was riding in a taxi with a stolid-faced driver who had not spoken to me as I climbed in. As we drove, I began to notice his unusual skill. By some trick of timing he seemed to miss all the red lights, and we flowed along with smooth speed.

At the end of the ride, I exclaimed involuntarily, "You're the best driver I've ever seen!"

The change in his face was startling. It was as if a light had been turned on inside. I realized that, almost without thinking, I had given him something he would value much more than the tip I offered: a sense of his own worth and the dignity of his profession.

Dear Father, Let me never forget that praise rightly earned should be given freely, for even those who serve through duty need to be encouraged. In Jesus' name, Amen.

Hospitality to Strangers

Do not neglect to show hospitality to strangers (Heb. 13:2).

A little girl who might have been condemned to a lifetime of suffering now has a chance to recover from her illness, thanks to a human chain of compassion. Five-year-old Guadalupe went through five agonizing cancer operations in her native Madrid, but all were unsuccessful. Her desperate parents spent their entire savings to bring her to the United States in the hope of finding a medical miracle.

When they landed at Kennedy airport they were penniless. A Spanish-speaking cabbie saw them, spoke to them, and heard their story. He took them, without charge, to a Hispanic neighborhood where he assured them they would find help.

As Guadalupe's parents wandered the streets, carrying her in their arms, they were approached by a well-to-do businessman who had noticed them trudging up and down for hours. He gave them shelter in his own home and then undertook to find the medical care the child needed.

When he called the executive director of a city hospital, the director immediately ordered a bed for Guadalupe. A team of doctors agreed to donate their services for the vital operation necessary, and the hospital provided all care without cost.

All who took part in this love-filled enterprise hoped that one day Guadalupe would laugh and play on the streets of Madrid, remembering that people in a land far away loved her as one of their own.

Dear Father, Help us remember that your people live in many places and that our love should extend to all. In the Savior's name, Amen.

Clearing the Way for Others

Let each of you look not only to his own interests, but also to the interests of others (Phil. 2:4).

In a supermarket one day, I felt buffeted by the thrusting crowd of shoppers. I had the depressing sense that everyone was blocking the path of others or trying to push ahead of his rightful place in line.

Then I noticed a young mother, who was speaking to her daughter aged about six.

"When we have to stop, dear, pull the cart over to one side so it won't block the aisle. Other people want to get through, too, you know."

My spirits lifted. The cheering thought came to me that life in the future will be much pleasanter for a lot of people because of what that little girl is being taught today. She is learning that in the pressure to fulfill our own needs we must not forget the consideration due to others.

Dear Father, As I go about the business of my life day by day, let me never forget that I am not alone in having needs and purposes to fulfill. Make me willing to clear the way for others so that their tasks may become easier because of me. In Jesus' name, Amen.

Called to Drive a Bus

The joy of the Lord is your strength (Neh. 8:10).

I've always remembered a scrawny little man called Johnny, whose last name I never knew. He was a bus driver in a town where I was once employed.

Everyone in town knew and loved Johnny. Climbing onto his bus was like entering a world of goodwill and happiness. He greeted each rider with a smile and a cheery "Good morning!" or "Good afternoon!" He leaped from his seat to help disabled passengers aboard. He never tired of giving minute directions to strangers.

I was riding his bus one day when I looked out the window and saw a young mother and short-legged toddler trying frantically to reach the corner before the bus stopped. I knew they'd never make it, and I felt a pang of sympathy; it was a cold day, and they'd have a fifteen-minute wait for the next bus. The bus company rules forbade drivers from waiting for tardy passengers.

There was a sudden screech of brakes, and the bus ground to a halt right in the middle of the long block. The door opened, and the grateful mother boarded with her child.

I think, whether consciously or not, Johnny regarded his job as a calling. Like a minister of God, a brilliant surgeon, or an inspired teacher, he made life better for many. He had found the Source of joy, and it flowed through him to others.

Dear Father, Let me be conscious always of the joy I should feel in knowing you, so that my happiness can be reflected for others. In Jesus' name, Amen.

To Tell the Truth

Let your light so shine before men, that they may see your good works and give glory to your Father who is in heaven (Matt. 5:16).

When I was in high school I had a classmate named Polly, a gentle, deeply religious girl. Polly seemed like an idealized character out of a novel, too good to be true. Yet none of us who knew her ever doubted that her goodness was real. She was as near the divine as a human being can be.

One day another member of the class decided to play a prank on our English teacher. When she called on him for the assignment of the day he opened his eyes wide and said, "But Miss G., you didn't ask us to prepare that." Several of his friends, who had been primed, spoke up to agree with him.

The rest of us caught on quickly and joined the game. One after another, thinking it a great joke, we declared that we remembered no such assignment.

Our teacher, poor lady, was first bewildered and then suspicious.

After awhile, she swiveled in her chair and her eyes rested on Polly.

"Polly," she said, "did I or did I not make that assignment?"

I saw color rise in Polly's face and her expression of deep distress. But without a moment's hesitation she replied, "Yes, Miss G., you did."

A small ripple of laughter passed around the room, followed by a thoughtful silence. Perhaps all my classmates were thinking, as I did, what an amazing grace it was to be so incorruptible that someone can seek truth from you with the certainty that it will be given.

Nobody ever called Polly a snitch or a goody-goody. We knew that a goody-goody is someone who enjoys feeling morally superior and is glad to reveal the faults of others. Polly felt pain rather than pleasure in causing discomfort to her classmates, but faced with a choice she could not lie.

Truth became more beautiful for everyone whose life she touched.

Dear Father, Help me to be incorruptible with humility, good without being judgmental, always as kind as it is possible to be but never shrinking from the course that I believe is right. In Christ Jesus' matchless name, Amen.

No Leftouts in My Class

Find grace to help in time of need (Heb. 4:16).

Each year the Elks' Lodge in my hometown gives a Christmas party for children who would otherwise have no part in the festivities of the season. There are always gifts, a Christmas tree, Santa Claus, the singing of carols, and the reading of the Christmas story from the Scriptures.

I had never fully realized the importance of this program until one holiday season when the children in the class I taught began chattering about their Christmas plans. The boys and girls from affluent homes soon made it a tale-topping session, telling about the wonderful gifts they expected, the towering trees they would have in their living rooms, the feasts to be enjoyed, and the visits to be made.

I became uneasy, fearing that the poorer children would feel left out. But just as I began to steer the conversation into what I felt would be less hurtful channels, Albert spoke up happily, "Well, I'm invited to the Elks' Christmas party."

Several other children quickly broke in to announce that they, too, would be guests on that happy occasion. I breathed a sigh of relief. There were no leftouts in my class.

Christmas would be a time of wonder for them all because a group of thoughtful men cared.

Dear Father, Bless all those who help to make Christmas a beautiful time for children. Let them feel the joy they give and understand that its Source is you. In Jesus' name, Amen.

I Wore a Blessing

The Lord will be your everlasting light, and your days of mourning shall be ended (Isa. 60:20).

Once during my college days when I had a very special date, several of my friends gathered to decide what I should wear for the happy occasion. It was our custom in the house to pool our "best dresses," trading clothes freely so that all of us would have a variety of changes.

As I was offered dress after pretty dress, Jane came forward and said, "Try this one."

I looked at it and shook my head. "Oh, no, Jane, I couldn't. You haven't had a chance to wear it yourself, and I know you bought it especially for when Bill comes."

"He isn't coming." Jane couldn't quite meet my eyes. "He isn't coming at all anymore."

Seeing the hurt look on her face, I asked no questions, but as I slipped my arms rather reluctantly into the dress I realized that something rather wonderful had just happened. At the time of her own sorrow, Jane had wanted my happiness to be as complete as possible.

It is not hard to be generous when fortune has smiled on

us. We want to share our joy. But to be glad for another during a time of personal pain is the gift of a rare spirit.

My friends decided that Jane's dress was the one I should choose. When I wore it that night I felt as if I had put on the blessing of a generous heart.

Dear Father, Let me never be so blinded by pain that I cannot rejoice that others have been made glad. Let me contribute to their happiness in any way I can even at the time of my heartache. In Jesus' name, Amen.

A Pat on the Back

Let us consider how to stir up one another to love and good works . . . encouraging one another (Heb. 10:24-25).

Some years ago an ice storm of major proportions struck my hometown, leaving a shambles of destruction, including downed electrical wires and the cutoff of service.

While linemen slogged through icy drifts locating trouble spots and repairing damage, the telephone at the local company office rang with a constant stream of complaints. "Why haven't you finished the repairs? My food is spoiling without refrigeration!" "Are you asleep up there? I'm losing business without lights!"

When service was restored, the community drew a collective sigh of relief. But one couple, a kindly doctor and his wife, did more. They sat down and wrote a letter to the electric company manager which stated, in part: "Thank you for putting in so many extra hours to restore our service. We saw the young linemen working in freezing wind and knew the risk they ran from live wires hidden under the snow and rubble."

52

One of the linemen said, "I was feeling pretty bitter until that letter came. Now I'd gladly go through it all again."

We have a habit of being harshly critical of the utilities that are the caretakers of our comfort. We see them as soulless, disembodied organizations. But behind the impersonal facade are men and women whose work, often hard and grueling, gives us the ease we cherish. A pat on the back can sometimes be more heartening than a bonus.

Dear Father, Let me never take for granted the amenities I enjoy, but rather teach me to remember the providers with gratitude and praise. In Jesus' name, Amen.

"Saving Face" for Others

Blessed are the merciful, for they shall obtain mercy (Matt. 5:7).

Miss M. was in her bank buying travelers' checks. The young woman teller instructed her to sign each check in two places. Miss M. hesitated, always before having used checks on which the second signature was to be made only when a check was cashed. However, the teller was firm, and Miss M. concluded that the rule had been changed.

As she was signing the checks a supervisor came by and saw what she was doing.

"Madam," he said icily, "you have made these checks useless by making the second signature here. They will have to be cashed immediately, and you will need to buy new ones."

His tone was so scornful that Miss M. felt her anger rising. She was about to retort that one of his own employees had instructed her on how to sign, but before

53

the words were out she caught a glimpse of the young teller's face. The teller wore an expression of abject terror.

Obviously, the woman was new on the job. She had made a serious mistake, and her boss was about to find out. Miss M.'s annoyance turned to sympathy. A supervisor who could be so rude to a customer would no doubt be merciless in judging the errors of an employee. He might even fire her, and jobs were in short supply.

Miss M. said calmly, "Well, it seems a mistake has been made, so let's start again."

It is human to want to save face for ourselves, but sometimes the spirit of mercy suggests that we let another's mistake go unnoticed.

Dear Father, Give me the grace to spare others pain when I can, even protecting them from too-harsh penalties for honest mistakes. In Jesus' name, Amen.

Sharing That Breaks Boundaries

The earth has yielded its increase; God, our God, has blessed us (Ps. 67:6).

As a teenager, I used to pass a certain house every day on my way to school. I only slightly knew the people who lived there.

One day as I was going by, the woman of the house came to the fence and called to me. She was carrying a beautiful pink rose she offered me.

"My garden has so many flowers this year," she said. "I thought I'd like for you to have this one."

I thanked her, feeling pleased but a little puzzled. I

wondered why she had felt the impulse to share her garden with someone who was almost a stranger. Yet without understanding I knew the gift had made my day brighter, giving me a feeling of greater self-worth because I had been so favored.

It took many years to make me comprehend fully what that woman must have felt on that bright spring day, but I have since experienced it myself. When God's world is particularly lush with natural beauty, our hearts open with the desire to share. We offer plump, red tomatoes from a garden patch to a neighbor, or carry peaches from our farm to a friend in town, or invite someone to enjoy a cookout in our backyard. Perhaps, imagination carrying us to places we have never seen, we write a check to help feed hungry people we have not met.

It is a way of saying, "I am so happy because of all the goodness which has been given me that I want others to be happy, too."

Dear Father, Thank you for the bountiful earth that opens our hearts with gladness and the kind impulse to share. Let us remember, at these happy times, that our sharing needs to break boundaries, so that your largess may bless all people. In Jesus' name, Amen.

Clippings of Grace

As each has received a gift, employ it for one another, as good stewards of God's varied grace (1 Pet. 4:10).

A retired woman who was unable to take part in activities requiring physical exertion decided to make clipping her hobby. After reading her newspapers and magazines she went through them carefully, cutting out items that might have interested people who did not subscribe to those publications. Articles on gardening, science, health, and many other subjects were culled. These were sent to friends and acquaintances by mail or delivered in person. Particular attention was given to providing material for shut-ins, and this led to the making of scrapbooks of cutout pictures for the use of children in hospitals.

One housebound woman whom the retiree had favored with her clippings said in amazement, "I met that woman only once in my life! To think she remembered that my hobby is old buttons!"

To remember the special needs and interests of other persons is to tell them in heartwarming ways that you recognize their uniqueness as human beings.

Dear Father, Wherever I am and whatever my situation, help me to discover what I can do to give joy to others. For Christ's glory, Amen.

Look for the Lonely Person

Encourage the fainthearted, help the weak (1 Thess. 5:14).

The chaperon at a church, youth-group program noticed a rather unattractive, overweight girl sitting alone, not taking part in the fun the others were having.

Her first impulse was to say to some of the youngsters, "Go over and talk to Mindy, won't you? Ask her to join in the games." On second thought, this didn't seem to be a good idea. Mindy was shy and self-conscious, but she was not stupid. She would probably recognize the gesture as an act of pity.

A better idea came. The chaperon walked over and said briskly, "You play the piano, don't you, Mindy?"

Mindy looked up, misery clear on her face. "Yes, Ma'am."

"Fine! I want to get the group around the piano for a round of singing, so I need your help."

Although Mindy began her chore hesitantly, by the end of the evening she was laughing and relaxed. She was the center of attention as boys and girls called out the titles of their choice songs. Without effort, she was one of the crowd.

It isn't always easy to help a shy person relax, but perhaps the surest way is to make him feel needed.

Dear Father, When fun is most intense, let mine be the eye which sees the lonely person on the edge of the crowd. Show me the best way to bring him into the circle of happiness. In Jesus' name, Amen.

A Quarter Multiplied

Maintain the rights of the needy (Prov. 31:9).

I have many happy memories of my father, a small-town grocer, but the recollection of one incident always brings tears to my eyes.

One day a fourteen-year-old girl came into his store and asked in a trembling voice, "How many groceries can I buy for a quarter?" (This was when a quarter was about the equivalent of today's dollar.)

Before he could reply, she burst into tears. Between sobs, she told her story: her father was out of work and in order to earn some badly needed food for the family she had hired herself out for housecleaning to a woman in the neighborhood. Being inexperienced, she did not bargain for her wages in advance, depending on the woman to pay her fairly. At the end of a long day of washing, scrubbing, and other hard chores, she had received a quarter.

My father assured her that the quarter would buy a "very large amount of groceries," and it did. When the girl left the store, she was carrying a basket filled several dollars' worth, enough food to feed a hungry family for days.

My father considered it a profitable transaction, not only for the girl but for him. He had been given the opportunity to right a wrong, and his own day had been made brighter by the glowing smile on the girl's face.

Dear Father, Help me not simply to rail against the wrongs committed by others but to set about transforming injustice by love. In Jesus' name, Amen.

A Cabbie's Turnaround

A soft answer turns away wrath (Prov. 15:1).

My boss, Dr. C., and several other employees, including me, were en route by taxi to meet a ship bringing us a visitor from England. This woman was on the staff of an organization in London related to ours, and we wanted to assure her a cordial welcome.

As we approached the pier the taxi driver, a dour-faced man, began to grumble. "I can't get you anywhere near that pier, or I'll get stuck in a jam of cars, and it'll take me an hour to get out."

He continued to mutter peevishly for the next block. Finally Dr. C., always a gentle person, spoke. "Well, sir, we certainly don't want to cause you any problems. I know how hard it is for a driver who gets caught in a traffic jam, so just get us as close as you can without any trouble to yourself, and we'll walk the rest of the way."

There was a moment of silence, and then the driver said, "Well, I'll do the best I can."

I watched the cabbie weave his way through the traffic, maneuvering us closer and closer to our destination. In the end, we were as close as we could possibly have been without driving aboard ship. As we left the cab, the driver gave us a smile and a wave.

I reflected that the passengers who followed us would probably find a pleasanter driver because Dr. C. had been patient and kind.

Dear Father, Help me always to remember the healing power of a soft reply to sharpness. In the holy name of Jesus, Amen.

The Prod of Conscience

My sin is ever before me (Ps. 51:3).

When a millionaire died recently, a surprising legacy was found in his will. Many years before, a stockbroker had mistakenly credited his account with $2,729. Being tempted by his need at the time, he remained silent and kept the money.

As time passed, however, his conscience troubled him more and more. In his will he specified that the full amount of the error, plus 6 percent interest, be returned to the broker.

"We have never seen anything like this before," exclaimed a member of the firm. "Talk about integrity. It restores your faith in mankind."

Conscience is a great nag, and we don't always enjoy its voice. But peace comes only when we listen.

Dear Father, When I have committed a wrong, let me set it right. Let me judge myself as sternly as I would judge others. In Jesus' name, Amen.

A Nameless Benefactor

When you give alms, sound no trumpet before you (Matt. 6:2).

The pastor and parishioners of a church in a changing neighborhood were struggling to keep their heads above a rising tide of expenses for which there were scant funds. The church had once thrived on the dues of a large and mostly affluent congregation, but as the neighborhood deteriorated many of the members moved away and transferred to other churches.

Those who remained wanted to continue where they were; for their new neighbors, though unable to make large financial contributions, needed the ministry of the church. Those who could increased their own giving, but the battle of upkeep seemed a losing one.

Then one day the pastor received a call from a lawyer. He had been asked to deliver a large check to the church from an anonymous donor. The man had heard of the church's plight and wanted to help. He refused to have his name disclosed, since he wanted no thanks.

This gift, sufficient to keep the church going until it could build up a new membership of small but steady contributors, saved a desperately needed ministry. The donor has remained nameless, but to all the members of the church, old and new, he is their beloved godfather.

Dear Father, Help me always to remember that what I give to the church is not for my glory, but yours. In Jesus' name, Amen.

A Never-forgotten Trust

The knowledge of the Holy One is insight (Prov. 9:10).

The weekly check I received from home during my college years was adequate but not lavish. I tried to spend my money carefully.

One week, just having cashed my check, I rushed to the university book store to buy a notebook. The store was crowded with jostling students, and tired clerks worked frantically to fill orders. When I was able to reach the counter and make my purchase, I took the change the clerk gave me and thrust it into my purse without looking at it.

That evening, when I started to pay for my dinner at the campus cafeteria, I realized that a mistake had been made. A ten-dollar bill was gone, and I had change for a five.

I agonized over what to do. I needed the lost five, but who would believe me?

Finally, shy and embarrassed, I returned to the store and approached the manager. He looked at me steadily as I told my story and asked, "Are you quite sure it was a ten you gave the clerk?"

I explained that since I had just cashed my check and had spent no money anywhere else I was very sure.

Without hesitation he opened the cash drawer and handed me five dollars, saying, "I like to think I can trust our students."

I have remembered that man with gratitude for many years. There is something about being trusted which gives one greater self-respect and the desire never to fail the expectations implied. Of course trust can sometimes be betrayed, but it seems to me better to trust too much rather than to trust too little.

Dear Father, Help me to trust in the goodness you have put into the nature of your creatures, hoping that where it has been corrupted my faith may help to restore it. In Jesus' name, Amen.

Miss R., Watcher of the Blinds

You shall love your neighbor as yourself (Matt. 19:19).

When my father died, my mother insisted on living on alone in the family home. This was a worry to her children, since all of us by then were living in other communities. Our concern was eased, however, by the simple undertaking of a young woman who lived nearby.

The windows of my mother's living room faced toward the street. Each night before she went to bed she lowered the blinds, and in the morning she raised them immediately after she rose. Miss R., who passed the house each morning on her way to work, offered to notice every day whether or not the blinds were up. If not (since she knew my mother was an early riser) she would investigate to see whether or not all was well.

Concern that our neighbors be "all right" is one expression of our kinship under God.

Dear Father, Teach me not to wait for the chance to do some great deed for my fellowmen but to remember that a small act of concern may have greater meaning than I realize. In Jesus' name, Amen.

Mr. Y.—Others Came First

Trouble and anguish have come upon me, but thy commandments are my delight (Ps. 119:143).

Many years ago my father had working for him a young man named Glenn. He had been orphaned at an early age and was brought up by a widowed grandfather, Mr. Y. The old man and the young had a close, devoted relationship.

When Glenn was drafted into military service, Mr. Y., like most relatives of servicemen, was wracked by anxiety. He used to come by our house often to talk with my father, who had recently been forced to retire from business because of a heart condition. Mr. Y. seemed to find comfort in these conversations, sometimes reading from Glenn's letters, because he knew my parents were fond of his grandson and shared his concern.

One day, trembling and pale, he appeared at the door, a paper clutched in his hand. When my mother admitted him, he asked whether or not my father's heart condition would make it dangerous for father to hear bad news. When my mother assured him she felt it would not be harmful, he let his grief be known. He had just received word that Glenn had been killed in action.

I don't think I shall ever cease to wonder at the courage and kindness of Mr. Y. His life shattered by the most terrible of sorrows, he considered my father's welfare before his own need for comfort. Only after my mother's reassurance did he allow himself to whisper, "My pal is gone," and let the tears fall.

Dear Father, When sorrow comes to me, as it does to all, let me not make it an undue burden for others but turn to you for the comfort my faith can offer in abundance. In Jesus' name, Amen.

Friendship Beyond the Call of Duty

There are friends who pretend to be friends, but there is a friend who sticks closer than a brother (Prov. 18:24).

A teenage drifter stood on the roof of a Bowery hotel, staring down fearfully at the street that yawned many stories below. Alone, friendless and miserable, he had determined to take his own life. He had only to make the plunge, and it would all be over.

"Take it easy, Son. You don't want to do this. You have a

lot to live for." A young police officer was edging toward him, careful not to move too quickly for fear of provoking the boy into a quick leap.

The boy took a step closer to the roof's edge. "I haven't anything to live for! Nobody loves me! Nobody cares!"

"I care." The officer spoke gently. "That's why I'm here. Come on, now. Come back with me, and let's talk it over."

The boy turned slowly and looked the officer in the face. What he saw there surprised him. The eyes were kind and concerned. The taut lines around the mouth indicated the strain of a man trying to save someone who was important to him. He looked as if he really did care.

Still the boy hesitated. Only after long persuasion did he hold out his hand and allow himself to be led to safety.

The officer realized that although the boy had been rescued from death he had not yet been introduced to life. He felt that the responsibility for this second step was his. A bachelor who lived alone, he decided to invite the boy to live with him and to apply for his adoption.

Today, thanks to the fact that someone cared, a would-be suicide looks forward eagerly to new life.

Dear Father, Thank you for all caring people and help me to be one of them. In Jesus' name, Amen.

Blessing from a Newsboy

I will bless the Lord at all times (Ps. 34:1).

During a period of recession, Mrs. B. and her husband were hard pressed to make ends meet. His business as a commercial artist had shrunk until it was almost nonexistent.

Despite her attempts to remain cheerful, Mrs. B. sometimes found herself feeling a little bitter. One day, noticing that there were threadbare spots on the covers of her sofa pillows, she rummaged through an old chest and found some remnants with which she made new covers. The new cloth, with its fresh designs, added a bit of brightness to the living room.

That afternoon when the newsboy came to deliver the evening paper he stared intently through the screen door at the refurbished sofa. A child from an impoverished home, he was a cheerful and friendly youngster.

"Those pillows sure are pretty," he commented. "You have the grandest house I ever saw."

Mrs. B. could hardly believe her ears. Her house grand, with its peeling paint and worn furniture? But she saw in the boy's big eyes that to him there was luxury in a home that was brighter than his own.

She felt a sense of shame. She had been feeling sorry for herself, when all around her there were others who needed her compassion.

"I've just baked some cookies," she said. "I'd like to give you some to take home."

In her prayers that night, Mrs. B. did not ask for a release from her problems, as she had so often before. She said a simple thank you to God for benefits already received.

Dear Father, Thank you for all the blessings you have bestowed upon me. Let me never forget that I have something to share with others. In Jesus' name, Amen.

Bypassing One's "Rights"

Better is a little with righteousness/than great revenues with injustice (Prov. 16:8).

Some years ago a young married couple I knew were killed in an automobile accident. Since they had no children, the question arose as to who should inherit the property they had owned together. The law provided that whichever of the couple had outlived the other should be presumed to have inherited the latter's share, and through him or her the property would pass to the next of kin.

In the hospital where they were taken following the accident it was determined that the husband had outlived the wife. This meant that his parents would be the inheritors.

When friends of the two families heard the news, they were shocked by the irony of it. The husband's parents were moderately wealthy, while the wife's parents were struggling with financial reverses.

However, the unfortunate circumstance was speedily resolved. The heirs quietly renounced claim to the property and asked that it be turned over to the family of their daughter-in-law. Thus, what could have been a legalized injustice became the occasion for an act of love.

For a number of reasons, wills can sometimes work unfairly. A faithful servant who was to have been rewarded may lose out because his employer has delayed changing an old will. A person drawing up a will may be incompetent.

Other unusual circumstances can arise. If the courts do not intervene, the heirs are faced with the choice of standing on their "rights" or of recognizing that such rights may actually be wrongs. In the case described above the inheriting parents chose the way of compassion and true justice.

Dear Father, Grant that I never claim my legal rights when they do not conform to the law of love. In Jesus' name, Amen.

How L. Learned to Read

I give you what I have (Acts 3:6).

In a retirement community on the Cumberland plateau in Eastern Tennessee, there is a nursing home which serves not only community residents but also people from the surrounding mountain neighborhoods. To this nursing home was brought L., an illiterate woman in her fifties. She had never been able to attend school because of a physical disability she had suffered from childhood. All her life she had longed to read, craving the knowledge and inspiration to be found on the printed pages of books. She spoke of her dream to doctors, nurses, everyone within earshot.

The story came to the ears of a woman in the retirement community who had been a professional in the field of education. She resolved to help L. For an hour a day, five times a week for three years, Mrs. G. tutored L. It was a delightful experience for both of them. L. had a fine mind which refused to be limited by her frail body. Her curiosity was unlimited, and every new word was a challenge. "What's this?" she'd ask, and then happily repeat the word that had been added to her vocabulary.

Today L. reads fluently, and her world of understanding is no longer limited by her handicap.

Although Mrs. G. was successful in her field before her retirement, teaching L. may well be her crowning achievement; for she gave the woman a key to the rich treasury of books. Like many other retirees, she knows that the opportunity for service does not end when we stop punching a time clock.

Dear Father, Help us remember that we remain instruments of your love until the last days of our lives. In Jesus' name, Amen.

A Volunteer Caretaker

Let us not love in word or speech but in deed and in truth (1 John 3:18).

In another community, far from the Cumberland plateau, a retired fireman has found a different way to serve.

When his active duties ended, Mr. M. looked around for ways to occupy himself. One day he went to a neighborhood park "to get out from under his wife's feet." He was appalled by what he saw. Glass, garbage, and dirty paper littered the grass and the playground intended for children.

"I felt sorry for all my friends and neighbors who couldn't use the park," he said, "so I just went to work."

Without salary Mr. M. took on the job of caretaker for the park. Year in and year out, rain or shine, he collects trash, trims the grass, and cleans latrines. He even does repainting of benches and lamp posts, and takes care of the playground and handball courts.

Neighbors are enthusiastic about his work. Youngsters

have a decent place to play and adults a restful haven in which to relax. One man who works in the area remarked, "There should be more like him. It would be a better world to live in."

Dear Father, You made the world beautiful, and I want to do my part to keep it that way. Help me remember. For Jesus' sake, Amen.

Intergenerational Sharing

Even a child makes himself known by his acts (Prov. 20:11).

Fifth-grade pupils in an Edgewood, Maryland, public school have carried out an unusual project. Learning about the nursing home in Tennessee where Mrs. G. taught L. to read, they decided to adopt the patients there as extra grandmas and grandpas. It has been an exciting venture. Letters are exchanged, and the youngsters send art work, tapes, and color photographs to their pen pals. In return, the oldsters send small craft items to the boys and girls.

For the men and women in the nursing home, the love and concern expressed by the youngsters affords both comfort and stimulation. The children, in turn, have learned that old people, even those so frail that they need special care, can still be interested in such things as stamp collections, music, games, family experiences, school activities, and even science-fiction stories. The knowledge will serve the kids well as they themselves move forward through time.

Dear Father, Help us all, whatever our ages, to be sympathetic to the needs and interests of those not of our own generation. In Jesus' name, Amen.

She Held Out for Acquittal

Keep your conscience clear (1 Pet. 3:16).

A woman wrote recently to a newspaper columnist with a plea that readers not try to evade their duty to serve on juries when called. She cited an experience of her own as an example of the need to meet this challenge in good conscience.

Some years ago she was summoned for jury duty at a time when it was inconvenient. She was tempted to duck, but could not reconcile this with her feeling of responsibility.

The case was a difficult one, and jury deliberations were exhaustive. Mrs. O. could not be convinced that the young man on trial was guilty, even though her fellow jurors felt that he was. She "held out" for acquittal despite their annoyance. Time after time one of them would urge, "Let us get this thing finished. I've got to get back to work!"

Mrs. O. begged the others to reexamine the evidence, and when they did they came to agree with her that no guilt had been established. They brought in a verdict of not guilty.

The life of the defendant since that time seems to bear out the correctness of the judgment. He has become a practicing lawyer with an exemplary reputation. Because one woman refused to violate her conscience with a hasty verdict, there is no blot on his record.

Dear Father, Let me always find time to serve in good conscience where I am needed. In Jesus' name, Amen.

"Mother of the Year"

Make a joyful noise to God, all the earth (Ps. 66:1).

Three of Mary Manachi's four children were born with the genetic blood disorder commonly known as "Cooley's Anemia," an affliction that prevents the body from properly manufacturing hemoglobin. For many years they and their parents commuted to a clinic where they received frequent hospitalization, regular blood transfusions, and sometimes surgery. It was a dreary and painful process, and one that offered no hope that the children could escape the early death for which they had been marked.

Despair might seem to have been the logical response to such a situation, but Mary Manachi never lost her belief that every life, however brief, should be celebrated and developed fully. She encouraged her children to participate in all the normal activities of childhood. They had hobbies, played musical instruments, and were active in their neighborhood church. They did well in school, and two of them entered college.

Mrs. Manachi did not hide the truth from them about their condition. She taught them to face it serenely and to be happy. She gave them her faith, and the solace she had found in the Bible.

Her courage reached out to help others who shared her tragedy. She organized trips for other children at the clinic and their families, encouraging them to savor the joy of each day they were given.

One of her children died in 1969 at age twelve, another in 1975 at age nineteen, and the third in 1980 at age nineteen. But Mary Manachi goes on, still visiting the clinic, a pillar of strength for those whose struggle has not ended.

One mother whose daughter is in the clinic said, "She's the one who gives us faith."

Mary herself has commented, "I learned to live my beautiful moments one day at a time."

When she was named "New Jersey Mother of the Year" for 1982, it was hardly more than a token recognition for a woman who had learned through faith to infuse her life and those of others with happiness in the face of adversity.

Dear Father, You have given us the gift of joy which we can claim at all times. Help us to hold it fast whatever our lives may bring. In Jesus' name, Amen.

The Cleaning Woman-Watchmaker

I bid every one among you not to think of himself more highly than he ought to think (Rom. 12:3).

Miss M. did not wear a wristwatch, so she kept a small clock on her office desk. One day she noticed that it had stopped running. Too busy to leave work just then, she determined to take it for repair the following day.

The next morning when she arrived at her office the clock was ticking away busily. Puzzled but pleased, she asked her co-workers who had repaired it. Nobody knew.

She worked late that evening and was still at her desk when the cleaning women arrived. One of them thrust a head inside her door and reported with a grin, "I saw your clock had stopped last night, so I fixed it for you."

Miss M. thanked the woman, but she was flabbergasted. This woman—this illiterate immigrant woman—had repaired her clock, a task she herself would have been helpless to perform.

She said later, "I got a big jolt of humility right then. I'm practically a moron when it comes to anything mechanical. I'd always supposed that woman wasn't even in my class when it came to brains, and here she was a lot smarter than I am in at least one respect. Ever since then I've been noticing all the things other people can do that I can't—the butcher who knows just how to cut the meat, the gardener with the green thumb, the coffeehouse cook who can handle a dozen orders at once, and so on. I guess we have to remember that God passed the talents around to a lot of people and didn't make any of us his special pets."

Of course Miss M. did not lose confidence in her own ability. Humility does not mean belittling our God-given gifts. It means respecting what others contribute and being willing to see all talents as part of the master plan in a world of give and take.

Dear Father, Thank you for the wonderful diversity of gifts you have given us. Let me use my own in service to you and my fellow-men and let me enjoy what others contribute in true appreciation. Through Christ our Lord, Amen.

A Cabbie's Lesson for Us

Every one helps his neighbor, and says to his brother, "Take courage!" (Isa. 41:6).

Knights who help ladies in distress did not vanish with the close of the Middle Ages. In our Christian culture today, without benefit of shining armor, they still dispense courtesy on the streets of our cities.

Recently when Miss H. parked her car, she absent-mindedly left the keys in the ignition switch and locked the doors. Some distance from the nearest service station, she felt helpless and distressed.

A passing cabbie saw her standing there and sensed that she was in trouble. He stopped and offered to help. Within a few minutes, using a wire, he was able to open the lock without damage. When Miss H. offered him ten dollars, he smilingly refused to take it.

Helping a friend is an act which seems natural even to some of the less generous among us. But for those whose hearts are open to the real meaning of fellowship there are no strangers; there are only neighbors to be served.

Dear Father, Help me to serve wherever I can, whenever I can, whoever I can. In Jesus' name, Amen.

"Mr. Kool"—Martyr for Kids

Who is wise and understanding among you? By his good life let him show his works in the meekness of wisdom (Jas. 3:13).

Several years ago two young policemen were gunned

down on the streets of New York. It was a senseless killing by a sniper who apparently hated all policemen and chose his victims at random.

The entire city was shocked by the crime, but in a neighborhood where one of the officers had counseled and coached young people there was particular grief. Eleven youngsters wrote a letter, "In memory of Patrolman Gregory Foster, 'Mr. Kool' to us," and left it at the funeral home where his body lay.

The letter read: "Mr. Kool, if I ever have the temptation of getting into trouble I'll close my eyes, and I'll believe I see you walking down the avenue as always, going into our clubhouse and asking us, 'Are you keeping kool, kids?'

"I'll always remember when you played basketball and baseball in the summer with us in the 12th Street park. I still have my glove, and I remember the last time you used it to pitch part of a game. Every time you heard about some kids in trouble you used to look for us and make sure that we had no part in it.

"I will always remember your last words to us; keep out of trouble, 'hey guys, stay kool.' We know that you are still with us walking down the avenue and keeping us kool. We'll miss you and never forget you, because we are sure you'll be beside us. From now on all the other cops will be 'Mr. Kool' to us but none as kool as you."

Mr. Kool's life was a short one, but the sniper's bullets could not destroy what he put into the hearts and minds of the boys for whom he cared so deeply. After all, the length of a life is not the important thing, but its quality.

Dear Father, Let me so live that when I am gone the world will be a better place because of me. In Jesus' name, Amen.

77

Put Actions to Your Words

Do not withhold good from those to whom it is due, when it is in your power to do it (Prov. 3:27).

When our fellow worker K. married M., a fine young man, all of us were happy for her. We enjoyed her wedding and admired the many nice gifts she had received, including our own.

K. and M. used their savings to furnish a modest but comfortable apartment and seemed set for a blissful honeymoon year. Then, one evening when they were away visiting friends, burglars broke in and took almost everything they had of value. It was a devastating anticlimax to a beautiful beginning.

For several days all of us in the office mourned. The whispers went around: "Isn't it awful?" "Those poor kids!" "What on earth will they do?" There were even a few dire mutters about what should happen to the thieves if they were caught.

Then one afternoon A. called us all together. "Look," she said, "it doesn't do a bit of good to keep saying how sorry we feel. Why don't we do something about it? It's almost Christmas time. We could take up a collection and replace some of the things K. and M. lost."

The idea was enthusiastically received, and cash began to flow. The fund raised did not, of course, replace everything which had been stolen, but it was enough to hearten K. and M. for the struggle ahead. More importantly, it let them know that when we said we were sorry we meant it.

Dear Father, Although it is not in my power to relieve all the hardships borne by others, help me remember to do what I can. In Jesus' name, Amen.

Jeanne—An "Angel of Mercy"

You have seen the purpose of the Lord, how the Lord is compassionate and merciful (Jas. 5:11).

Jeanne Daman, a young Christian woman, was a teacher in Brussels, Belgium, when the Nazis occupied her country during World War II. She was engaged to teach in a kindergarten set up by the Jewish community after the invaders refused to allow their children to attend the public schools. This gave her the opportunity to witness firsthand the appalling brutality of mass arrests which included even helpless youngsters.

Day after day boys and girls disappeared from her classroom, and she knew that they had been rounded up for shipment to prison camps with their parents. Sometimes gestapo officers came directly to the kindergarten and hauled the children away. Jeanne felt anguished but helpless.

Finally she decided that she must take action. Her school closed, and Jeanne took a secretarial position, but her real occupation was being a member of the Belgian underground particularly concerned with the rescue of Jewish children.

For two years she worked finding Christian homes for Jewish children, helping their parents hide, serving as a go-between for Jews and non-Jews.

Some of the families she asked to help were reluctant to get involved, realizing the danger to themselves. They would say, "We didn't want the Nazis. Are we responsible?"

Jeanne would reply, "No. Neither am I. But if, by silence, we allow a crime to happen without interference, then we are accomplices through our indifference. If you

79

don't keep this child, she will be taken away. If I come back after the war and tell you she is dead, you will feel guilt. Now you have a chance to do something."

Jeanne does not know how many children she personally saved, but in all of Belgium 2,000 were hidden away and escaped the camps. Many men and women living today recall the compassion that saved them.

Dear Father, We have been told that the merciful are blessed, and we pray for the grace never to look the other way when injustice is being committed among us. In Jesus' name, Amen.

Small Sacrifices

The good man out of his good treasure brings forth good (Matt. 12:35).

Diminishing funds made it necessary for the Department of Public Works in Plymouth, Michigan, to lay off one of its truck drivers. Mr. B. was the unfortunate man who received the pink slip. He told his thirteen co-workers good-bye and went home to break the bad news to his family. With jobs scarce and their bank account low, it looked as if they would soon be on welfare.

He had reckoned without the generosity of his colleagues. After he left, they talked things over, reached a decision, and went to city officials with a suggestion. If Mr. B. were kept on the job, each of them would take a week's vacation without pay.

Mr. B. was back on the job a week later. Overwhelmed with gratitude, he declared himself "almost speechless."

Thirteen families will have a little less, but one family will be saved from deprivation and the loss of security. The wonder of small sacrifices is that they so often achieve great purposes.

Dear Father, Make me willing to give up a luxury when it can buy another's necessity. In Jesus' name, Amen.

An Unusual Birthday Gift

He who pursues righteousness and kindness will find life and honor (Prov. 21:21).

It was September, and I was in a toy store following my usual custom of shopping early for Christmas. As I was examining some stuffed animals, a young man came up and stood beside me.

After a few minutes he selected a dog with big, bright glass eyes. "I think I'll take this one," he said, "he looks nice and frisky."

I commented, "I see I'm not the only one who shops early for Christmas."

"Oh, this isn't for Christmas," he said. "I'm buying it to give to my cleaning woman's little boy for my birthday."

"You mean his birthday," I corrected automatically.

He grinned. "No, *my* birthday. I always give somebody else a gift on my birthday. It's a habit my mother started for me when I was a kid. She'd bake a big cake for me every year and when we were eating it with ice cream, she'd say, 'Now who would you like to give a present for your birthday?' She'd steer me into thinking of someone who didn't have as many toys and other things as I did. It was a lot of fun, and I've kept it up."

He picked up the dog and started walking jauntily toward the checkout counter. He seemed like a happy man, and why not? Happiness is one thing we can never entirely give away. It always comes back.

Dear Father, Help me remember to share my happy moments in love and thankfulness for all I have been given. In Jesus' name, Amen.

Mary's Daily Concert

The fruit of the Spirit is love, joy, peace, patience, kindness, goodness, faithfulness (Gal. 5:22).

When my friend Mary was in high school, she lived next door to an elderly blind man whose greatest pleasure lay in music. He had an old-fashioned phonograph and a set of records that he liked to hear played over and over again. Since he could not see the titles on the records and it was difficult for him to operate the machine, he needed help to enjoy his favorite pastime. Mary made it her commitment to give him a daily concert. Although she was a lively girl, interested in a variety of activities, she never let anything interfere with her visits to Mr. M.

Sometimes, when Mr. M. received his monthly pension check, he sent Mary to the music store to select a new record for him. On one of those occasions, she asked me to go with her. I noticed that she made no hasty selection, as if eager to have done with the chore. Instead, she considered a number of records. Head to one side she would listen, shake her head, and comment, "No, I don't think he'd like that one." Then finally, smiling, she nodded. "Yes, I think this is the right one."

It's been a long time since that day, but I still remember the happy smile on Mr. M.'s face as, hands and feet keeping time to the music, he listened to a record that had been chosen for his special pleasure.

Dear Father, Let me not forget to give pleasure when I can, and let my offering be chosen with sensitivity and love. In Jesus' name, Amen.

The Best Mother's Day Gift

Let your father and mother be glad, let her who bore you rejoice (Prov. 23:25).

When Mother's Day approached, Angie lamented to a friend, "What can I do? John's out of work, the rent's due, and the grocery bill has to be paid. I can't possibly buy a Mother's Day gift, but I love my mother like crazy. I hate to settle for some silly card."

Her friend replied, "Why not write her a letter and tell her how much you love her? I think she'd like that."

Angie thought it over, and the idea grew in her mind. At last she sat down and wrote:

"Dear Mother, Mother's Day is coming, and I'd like to buy you something fabulous, like maybe a beautiful four-wheel-drive car or a mink coat or a diamond as big as a doorknob. But my purse is flat, so I decided to do the next best thing: write and tell you that I love you very much.

"I remember how you were always ready to offer comfort when I needed it like the time when I'd lost two front teeth, and some girls told me I was the ugliest kid in school. I was almost hysterical by the time I got home, but you just hugged me and said that to you I was the prettiest girl in the whole world. And of course you always told me how proud you were when I made good grades or did something like getting on the girls' drill team. I don't think anyone ever had a kinder or more understanding mother. So please believe me when I say I love you more than I can express. Your doting daughter, Angie."

In due time, Angie received the following reply:

"My darling Angie, You didn't do the next best thing. You did the very best thing. I've never craved a big car, a mink coat, or a flashy diamond. But like most normal human beings, I sometimes need to hear that I am loved. It is one of the most beautiful gifts anyone can give or receive. Thank you with all my heart. I love you, too. Mother."

Dear Father, Teach me to speak of love whenever the words can bring happiness to those who have my affection. In Jesus' name, Amen.

Three Half-pints

So then, as we have opportunity, let us do good to all men (Gal. 6:10).

Uncle Lee was a reasonably affluent retiree, able to indulge himself in small pleasures. After the death of his wife he developed the habit of walking each summer afternoon to a nearby grocery to buy a half pint of ice cream. He would sit down at the kitchen table and eat it slowly, savoring each bite.

On his way to and from the grocery he had to pass a pocket-sized neighborhood park. He began to notice that two rather wretched-looking old men were always there, sitting on a bench in the one spot of shade the park provided. There were rooming houses in the area, and Uncle Lee speculated that the bench sitters must live in one of them. He knew what some of those single-room residences were like: hotboxes in which a human being could only swelter and look at the walls. The old men had probably escaped to the one place where they could hope for slightly cooler air.

On his next trip to the grocery, Uncle Lee bought three half pints instead of one. Two of them were delivered to the old men in the park, with the offhanded remark, "Awfully hot today. Thought you fellows might like to have something cool."

He had expected a polite thank you but was amazed by the almost ecstatic enthusiasm with which his gift was received. It made him aware that even small treats must be rare in the lives of these men. After that, for the rest of the summer, there were always three portions of ice cream.

Uncle Lee was always a generous man. His gifts to the church and to charities were numerous. As a child I learned that he delighted in slipping coins into the hands of small nieces and nephews. Once when I was in the hospital he bought a beautiful doll to place beside me on the bed. But I doubt if the warmth of his great heart was ever better expressed than it was that summer when he made the hot days more tolerable for two old men with a treat of ice cream.

Dear Father, Help me remember the importance of thoughtfulness in little things, for sometimes small kindnesses are great in the lives of others. In Jesus' name, Amen.

Mrs. B.'s Brochure

And let us not grow weary in well-doing (Gal. 6:9).

Mrs. B. felt anxious and depressed when she went into the hospital for treatment of a broken hip that was refusing to heal. For the first several days of her stay she wondered fearfully: Will they be able to help me? Do these people really care about me as a human being?

Gradually her mood changed. She saw that the staff of the hospital was not only efficient but that the doctors and nurses all seemed to be caring persons. One day she asked one of the nurses, "Will my hip ever heal?" When the woman replied, "You'll walk out of here," the warm smile that accompanied the words gave Mrs. B. new heart.

With her own tension eased, she began to notice newly arrived patients. Most of them looked as anxiety ridden as she had been. Whenever she had the opportunity, she spoke reassuringly to them. It seemed sad that they and all the patients who would come to the hospital in the future could not have the comfort of knowing in advance the kind of care they would receive.

Mrs. B. had experience as a writer of promotion copy. She drafted a description of the hospital's procedures, facilities, personnel, and spirit and presented it to the administrator with the suggestion that it be printed as a brochure for prospective and incoming patients. He was delighted and grateful.

Now, because one woman viewed her ordeal as an opportunity, others can face hospitalization with more ease of mind.

Dear Father, Help me to see any opportunity for service that may arise and use such gifts as I have to meet it. In Jesus' mighty name, Amen.

The Bag Woman's Real Identity

As you did it to one of the least of these my brethren, you did it to me (Matt. 25:40).

She was a bag lady on the streets of Miami Beach, Florida, one of those pathetic, homeless women who wander from place to place carrying with them whatever they own. She dressed in rags, slept on the beach, and ate anything she could find or beg.

Now and then she told a fantastic story. She said she belonged to a well-to-do English family and had come to the United States several years before for a temporary stay. Shortly after her arrival she had been mugged and beaten. The thief had stolen all her money and her identification cards. The beating had left her so dazed that for a time she was unable to communicate coherently, and by the time she began to recover she had become part of the city's seedy underworld.

Those who heard her story sighed sadly and shook their heads. They knew how easily illusions grew in dazed minds. So they offered a few coins and passed on.

Then one day she went to a community center to ask for help. A counselor there listened in wonder to her tale. She recognized something of dignity and intelligence in the woman's manner. Could her story possibly be true? It seemed unlikely, but the social worker was a sympathetic and conscientious woman. She determined to make sure.

She sent an inquiry to the British consulate in Atlanta, Georgia, and the staff there soon established the woman's identity. Her story was true! They found that her family, after an earlier search, had given her up for dead. Now she is back home again, receiving the loving care that it is hoped will make it possible for her to recover from her nightmare.

Dear Father, Keep me always attentive when someone confides his woes, for I may be just the person he needs to help solve his problem. In Jesus' name, Amen.

Fear Turned to Courage

When I am afraid, I put my trust in thee (Ps. 56:3).

W., a seventeen-year-old young man, was walking along the street one evening when his attention was arrested by the sight of flames shooting from the upper-floor windows of a house he was passing. He began to shake uncontrollably. All his life he had been particularly terrified of fire, of being burned to death.

He looked around desperately for help, but no one else was in sight. He knew there must be people in the house, and if he ran away to give the alarm help might come too late to save them. Without hesitation he plunged forward, broke through the front door, and groped his way through the smoke-filled hallway. In a first floor bedroom he found an elderly couple asleep, woke them, and led them to safety.

Then, to his horror, he learned that another man was in bed on the second floor. Again he braved the smoke and flames, this time joined by a second passerby.

The house had become an inferno. Three times the rescuers were driven back by heat so intense W. could feel it burning through his jacket. Frantic efforts to break through to the trapped man ended in defeat.

When firemen arrived and W. tried to explain his actions, he wept. "I don't know what came over me. I just didn't want him to burn to death."

Unknowingly, W. had reached beyond his own weakness to the God-given resource of true courage. All of us, at some time in our lives, face fear. It is not always fear of physical danger; it may be fear of social censure if we follow conscience against popular opinion or fear of failure in some worthwhile venture. But if, like W., we go forward with the needed action, courage will come.

Dear Father, Save me from cowardice; gird me with courage even in the face of certain hurt. In Jesus' name, Amen.

The Remover of Tattoos

A new heart will I give you, and a new spirit I will put within you (Ezek. 36:26).

Among some youthful gang members who want to project the image of being tough and dangerous, a common practice is to have themselves tattooed with pictures and slogans which advertise their bravado. Arms and hands may wear snarling tigers, sinuous snakes, or such words as "Born to raise _____."

With the passing of years, some of these youngsters take a sober second look at their lives and decide to rejoin society. The tattoos then become an embarrassment and a hindrance. Prospective employers look at the disfigured skin and shake their heads. They are reluctant to hire someone who looks as if he might blow up the plant or rob the till.

Having tattoos removed surgically is an exhorbitantly expensive process. Without a job, the would-be employee has no money to pay for it. In desperation he may be tempted to go back to his old life.

A surgeon has been devoting two days a month to help these young people, operating on them without charge. He makes sure that they really intend to put their past behind them and checks to see that their parents approve. He then proceeds, and thus far has removed seventy-five of the stigmatizing marks.

The good doctor is surely an instrument of God as he helps those whose hearts have been changed to rid themselves of the outer evidence of past mistakes.

Dear Father, Bless everyone who holds out a hand to help those who have erred and grant that I, too, may extend such charity whenever I can. In Jesus' name, Amen.

The Crippled Cops

Never flag in zeal, be aglow with the Spirit, serve the Lord (Rom. 12:12).

The town of Capitola, California, has found a way to

employ crippled men and women in constructive jobs that serve both them and the community. Sitting in their wheelchairs, they act as parking cops.

The unusual experiment has been an astonishing success. Macho drivers who might argue with a burly policeman, or even throw a punch when ticketed, respond politely when a man or maid in a wheelchair puts the unwelcome slip under the windshield. Passersby sometimes rush to help one of the seated cops when they see the person is having trouble reaching a high wiper blade.

The police chief, who started the program, says, "Some fine people who might not get a chance anywhere else now have useful, adventurous jobs, and our town has found some great workers. Everybody wins."

One of the wheelchair-bound cops points out the lack of friction between the officers and the public. "We get more friendly smiles and kind words than all the other parking police in the country put together."

No doubt the sight of crippled persons working cheerfully to support themselves inspires admiration and respect in all but the most hardhearted. It is good to hear about a community with so much imagination and heart.

Dear God, We thank you that you are leading us increasingly to recognize the contributions that can be made by those who are physically handicapped. In Jesus' name, Amen.

Retarded Is Just a Word

We love him, because he first loved us (1 John 4:19).

When Mr. P. was a small boy, a doctor told his mother that he should be institutionalized, since he was so severely retarded that he would never be able to lead a normal life. He spent his childhood in a home for the mentally handicapped because, as he says, "they'd given up on me."

Finally, however, a wise and kind counselor took the time to talk with him and learn to know him. He was convinced that Mr. P. could live outside the institution and hold a job, and he took steps to make it possible. "He saved my life," says Mr. P.

Now twenty-nine, he has a janitorial job and lives in his own apartment. He cooks and shops for himself and enjoys community recreation. Last summer he went camping with a group that specializes in arranging trips for the mentally retarded. He was thrilled by his first rowboat ride.

Life is very full for him now. He doesn't worry because he isn't one of the world's smartest people. The compassion of those who didn't give up on him has made it possible for him to comment, "Retarded is just a word; they can say it all they want, but I just let it pass me by."

Dear Father, Help us remember that the less gifted are also your children and should never be denied the abundance of life. In Jesus' name, Amen.

Lummie's Loss Was a Gain

O death, where is thy victory?
O death, where is thy sting? (1 Cor. 15:55).

My Great-aunt Lummie lived at some distance, so I never really knew her. However, the story of her conversion was one of my mother's favorite family reminiscences, and I heard it when I was quite young.

Aunt Lummie was a handsome woman with a bright mind but very little interest in things of the spirit. She went to church on Sunday because that was what nice people in her community did, but her attendance was more of a social gesture than a commitment.

The softer side of her nature was expressed almost solely in the adoration she lavished on her only daughter, Kate. To everyone's surprise Kate grew up to be a deeply religious young woman, a Christian so devout that her personality seemed to radiate her faith. Aunt Lummie accepted her daughter's dedication with a sort of loving tolerance.

Then, in the first bloom of young womanhood, Kate became ill. Her illness was a terminal one, and Aunt Lummie watched her beloved daughter move slowly toward death.

On the final day, she sat by Kate's bedside, torn with grief, keeping watch. Kate, still conscious, was serene. Softly, she quoted comforting passages of Scripture.

When her voice trailed away and the doctor determined that her life had at last ended, Aunt Lummie leaped to her feet, weeping and crying out in anguish, "Oh, my darling! I've lost you forever!"

Immediately, from close beside her where no one stood, she heard a voice say quite distinctly, "No, not forever."

Skeptics who hear Aunt Lummie's story find a psychological rather than a spiritual explanation for her experience, but Aunt Lummie never doubted, then or later, that the voice was from outside herself. It changed her life. From that day on, she became as devout as her daughter had been. She took up the study of the Scriptures and declared that she found in them answers to her own problems and those of others.

All of us, unless we are among the few who die very young, sooner or later lose someone we love. The experience can be bitter, tearing us apart emotionally, but it need not be. It can, instead, bring a deepening of faith as we open our hearts to the Source of comfort.

Dear Father, Grant me the grace to meet the death of those I love not with undue sorrow but with thankfulness for the love I have had and with confidence that what you have created is eternal. In Jesus' name, Amen.

How Love Is Given

I know how love is given:
A thousand lovely ways
That bless each passing moment
And glorify our days;
For eyes that see our sorrow
And hearts that feel our pain
Reflect divine compassion
To make us whole again;
And happiness increases
When joy is passed along,
For each believer's paean
Becomes a choral song.

Pray God that we remember
The common fate we share
Of hurt and hope and struggle
With people everywhere
And hold to faith as members
Within the cosmic plan
That finds its perfect pattern
In love of God and man.

About the Author

Mae Hurley Ashworth is an accomplished writer and former editor, now semiretired and continuing her freelance writing. She has been an editor with David C. Cook Publishing Company and the Friendship Press.

She has published five books and a number of dramas, filmstrip scripts, and puppet scripts. She has also published hundreds of articles with magazines and journals, including *Seventeen, event, Teen Magazine,* and *Encounter.*

She lived in downtown Manhattan for many years and only recently relocated to Great Falls, Virginia.

About the Author